Were You Born In That Chair?

Jennifer Kuhns

Were You Born In That Chair?

All rights reserved
Copyright 2010 Jennifer Kuhns

This is a work of fiction.
All characters and events portrayed in this book are fictional.
Any resemblance to real people is purely coincidental.

Reproduction in whole or part, in English or any other languages, or without the written permission of the author and publisher is strictly prohibited.

For information contact: Shalako Press
P.O. Box 371, Oakdale, CA 95361-0371
http://www.shalakopress.com

ISBN: 978-0-9798898-9-9

Cover Artist: Karen Borrelli
Editor: Rofiah Breen
All art and illustrations contained in this book are by Karen Borrelli

shalako press
www.shalakopress.com

PRINTED IN THE UNITED STATES OF AMERICA

Acknowledgments

Rofiah Breen, my favorite "retro hippie chick," thank you for treating me as no less than your equal as a writer, listener, confidante, and human being. I wholly appreciated your Point of View (POV), while you mentored and helped me hone my writing skills as well as during the process of your editing my book, and accepting my choice not to agree with every suggestion.

Louise Loots, thank you for giving me that two-page creative writing assignment during my first semester at Gavilan College—an assignment that has evolved into so much more, and for suggesting that a talent may be unfolding and revealing itself.

Mark Levine, a second Gavilan professor. Disability classified as a multicultural group, who would have thought? Thank you for being first to share my story.

On a personal level and most importantly, I must thank my family members for their unwavering support. They have given me the opportunity to grow, share and be a contributing and equal member of our family. Thank you for letting me be part of your lives and using those experiences to fuel my heart, my imagination, and my determination.

Last, but far from least, many thanks to all who read and responded to my manuscript, the teachers, the children and the parents. Your feedback confirmed my belief that there was truly a need for my story to be heard.

DEDICATION

I would like to dedicate the publication and release of *Were You Born in that Chair?* to two people, Marco, whose last name long forgotten, set the ball rolling by innocently and persistently demanding an answer to his question. Second, to Nicole Salinas, my childhood friend and physical therapy partner who was taken too soon (1982-1995).

Were You Born In That Chair?

It was seven forty-five in the morning and Hailey spent the last few minutes she had fussing with her hair and putting on her new purple sweater that already had her name tag pinned to it while she waited for her mother to drive her to school. Hailey's hair was blonde, a little longer than shoulder length and was just beginning to get caught on the headrest of her wheelchair, but she was determined to let it keep growing. Her mother had agreed to let her try as long as it didn't just hang and get in the way. So Hailey was extra careful about keeping her head up and her hair pulled back and out of her face.

Hailey was excited and nervous at the same time since it was the first day of a new school year at a new school. She had always gone to a school where she had known all the children and being in a wheelchair was not a big deal. At her old school everyone, all the students, had some kind of limitation or obstacle to conquer. She had learned sign language because some of the children couldn't hear or speak. Others were blind, so the whole class had to learn how to tell time by using snack time plates as clocks. The applesauce was at three o'clock, the muffin was at nine o'clock and the milk was above the plate at two o'clock. Hailey had not been the only one in a wheelchair. There had been several other students in wheelchairs and walkers, so she never felt weird or out of place. She was going to miss all of her old classmates and friends, but today she was going into the third grade at a new school where she would meet new people and make new friends.

As Hailey and her mother pulled up into the school parking lot in the van that was made especially for people in wheelchairs to ride in, Hailey began to feel a knot growing in her stomach. All of a sudden she found that she was more nervous than she was excited. Hailey noticed that her mother could tell that she was a little squeamish about her first day at the new school. Hailey was also aware that her mom was maybe a bit anxious, too. As Hailey's mother unloaded her from the van and wanting to make the change to a new school easier for her daughter, she offered to walk her to class.

    "No thanks, Mom. I can do this by myself." Hailey answered as she drove her wheelchair toward the playground. "I'll see you after school."
    Her mother walked back around to the driver's side of the van and

got in. She sat in the parking lot for a few minutes until Mrs. Lacey, Hailey's new teacher, waved to let her know that she saw Hailey coming. Hailey's mom took a deep breath and gave her daughter the help she needed by driving away as Hailey sat by the corner of a long row of classrooms and watched.

Children began to gather on the playground in front of the classrooms. Hailey's classroom was number eight, her lucky number. She saw a small group of children, who acted like they knew each other, stop in front of room eight. They seemed to be catching up with what went on during summer vacation. Hailey could hear them laughing and shouting all the way across the playground. Above their heads Hailey could see a lady, a teacher, standing in the doorway looking out at the children. Hailey noticed that the lady looked as worried as she felt.

"That must be my new teacher, Mrs. Lacey," Hailey whispered to herself.

Then she heard a loud voice coming from the other side of the playground. A boy named Blake was running toward a boy with red hair and freckles whose name tag read Simon.

"Hey dude, how'd you break your arm?" Blake excitedly asked Simon. "Are you in Mrs. Lacey's class?"

"Yeah, are you? I was hoping you would be 'cause you have the best Yugioh trading cards. Besides that, I don't know if I'll know anybody else and we can hang out together," Simon answered as he looked around the playground for anyone else he might know.

"Yeah, that'll be cool, but how did you break your arm?" Blake asked again.

Simon held up his right arm and shrugged his shoulders. "Well, we got a pool this summer. We spent lots of time swimming and stuff until Rita dared me to do a double back flip off of the diving board, and I broke my arm doing it." Blake looked at Simon's cast and thought for a minute. "How do you do stuff like tie your shoes if you can't use your arm?"

Simon laughed, "That's easy. Me and my dad went down to the shoe store and bought some shoes with Velcro, you know, that stuff that sticks to itself, so I don't have to tie them. But my mom has to help me comb my hair and I gotta wear T-shirts because I can't do the buttons by myself."

Blake shook his head, "That must really suck."

"Naw, it's not so bad. You kinda get use to it." Simon looked around and saw another boy he knew. "Hey look, there's Joel! Check it out! What's up with the hair?" Both boys turned and ran toward their friend.

When they reached Joel, Blake jumped back and pointed to Joel's head.

"Whoa, Joel, your mom let you dye your hair blue? My mom would never in a million years let me do that," Blake declared.

Joel reached up with both hands and touched the top of his head. He rubbed his hair thoughtfully and smiled. "Well, my mom didn't really let me do it." He paused, gave a little laugh, and then went on with his story. "She wasn't home one day, and my big brother wanted to test it out on me before he did his own hair so......" Joel trailed off. "Jeez, I've answered the same question so many times in the last couple of weeks that I'm really tired of telling it over and over again. I should have it on a CD or something so I could just hit a button and let it play.

I heard they were going to get new basketballs this year. Let's go check it out." The three boys agreed and headed for the ballroom, cutting through a dodge ball game.

The circle of children all screamed at the boys. "Hey you guys, get out of the way! Go around!"

"Sorry!" The three boys yelled at the same time as they continued, running past a group of girls playing jump rope.

"…blue bells, cockle shells, easy ivy, over. Hots! 1, 2, 3, 4, 5, 6, 7, 8,"

"You missed! Its Robin's turn," shouted a girl holding one end of the jump rope. Her name was Shelly.

Robin walked to the other end of the jump rope where Melissa stood holding onto the rope and asked. "Hey, Melissa, would you hold these for me so I don't drop and break them or something?"

"Yeah," Melissa answered as she reached out to take the glasses from Robin. "I'll put them here in my pocket." Melissa carefully slid the glasses into her shirt pocket and snapped it closed.

Satisfied that her glasses were safely in Melissa's pocket, Robin turned around to face the line of girls waiting to take their turn. "Hey, Rita, let's do twenty-four robbers."

"Sure. Ok." Rita stepped forward to join Robin. Rita was Simon's twin sister. "You start, and then I'll be the robbers and jump in."

"Cool. Ready?" Robin said as she began to jump, not waiting for an answer from Rita.

All of the girls began to sing as Rita waited for her cue to join Robin. "Not last night, but the night before, twenty-four robbers came knockin' at my door. As I ran out…" Robin then jumped out of the rope as Rita jumped in at just the right time and the girls carried on with their singing, "they came in…"

From across the playground the boys who had gone to check out the new ball supply went running past the girls jumping rope. They all shouted "Hi" to each other. When they had reached the ballroom, the boys discovered that all of the balls were gone. They had already been checked out by other students, so Joel, Blake and Simon started to fake dribbling and passing a ball. The boys made their way to an empty space on the blacktop area and began to play a pretend game of basketball. Blake was running backwards with his arms waving in the air, blocking Simon who was dribbling the imaginary basketball with his good arm. Joel was following, yelling at Simon to "go for it." Simon jumped to sink a three pointer. Blake was still running backwards trying to block Simon's shot and not looking where he was going.

Blake jumped too and came down slamming into something, making him lose his balance and fall. Surprised, but not hurt, Blake looked up from the ground at the person he had run into. He was sure that the other person had run into him so he started yelling.

"Hey, get out of the way! Watch out where you're goin'. We're trying to play a basketball game here. You gotta…OHHH!!!"

Blake and all of his friends backed away from what he had run into. Hailey grabbed onto the arms of her wheelchair, thinking that she had felt an earthquake or something. She was as shocked as Blake was acting. Hailey wasn't all that interested in basketball, so she hadn't been paying much attention to the boys, and didn't really see them coming. Hailey had been trying to make her way to the classroom door where her new teacher was standing and watching. The only person who had even seen her on the playground was her new teacher. No one else had seemed to notice that she was there, until the boy ran into her that is. Then all of a sudden everyone was noticing her. They were all staring at her like she had six eyes or something.

Hailey waited while Blake brushed the dirt off his new pants. She wasn't sure what to expect next. All Hailey knew was that the boy who ran into her had now stepped up in her face and was looking her up and down wearing an expression of interest and uncertainty. "Are you in the right school?" Blake asked in a voice that was louder than it needed to be. "I haven't seen you here before and I know everybody 'cause I've been here since kindergarten. What's the matter with you anyway? We don't have kids like you at this school. And how come you're in that thing? What, is it like a golf cart or scooter or something?"

Hailey took a deep breath. She had heard all of those same questions and lots of others many times before. Most of the time it didn't bother her, but today it did. She wasn't sure why it bothered her today, but maybe it was because she was at a new school and she was nervous. Or maybe it was because the kid yelling in her face was spitting on her new sweater when he talked. Hailey sat up as straight as she could and looked boldly into Blake's eyes and answered the only question that she could remember him asking.

"No, it isn't a scooter or something. It's a wheelchair. And you don't have to yell. I can hear."

No one said a word for what seemed like an hour to Hailey. She spent the whole time gazing at the red faced boy, waiting for a response. He spent most of the time either looking at the ground or around at his friends and the rest of the kids who were beginning to gather to see what all the noise was about.

"Oh, I just thought that maybe, ya know, you couldn't." Blake said in a more normal voice.

Mrs. Lacey hurried out of the classroom doorway where she had been watching and headed to where Hailey and the group of boys were standing. When Hailey spotted the teacher, almost running, she guessed that she wanted to stop any problems before they got out of hand. Hailey was sure that her new teacher was sort of nervous, too, and probably felt that she had to protect or stand-up for Hailey. Adults were always doing that, trying to save her from something or treating her like a baby.

Stepping in between them, Mrs. Lacey greeted Hailey. "You must be Hailey." She said. "I'm so pleased to finally meet you. My name is Mrs. Lacey, and I am going to be your third grade teacher."

Mrs. Lacey was a tall woman with short brown hair. She has a nice smile, Hailey thought to herself. She wore a long necklace that matched a bracelet that had bright colors and little tiny crayons on them.

"Hello," Hailey replied looking around and still feeling a little uneasy.

All of the children on the playground began to drift away from Blake and in the direction of Mrs. Lacey and Hailey. They formed a semi-circle around the two of them. No one said a word. They just stared, making Hailey feel uncomfortable.

A little afraid but angry now too, she looked around at the new faces staring at her and then looked back at Mrs. Lacey. "Why do people have to do that? Stare, I mean. How come they just can't see that I am pretty much like everyone else? Besides that is soooo rude!" Hailey stated more than asked. Then thinking for a minute she continued, "I bet they wouldn't like it if they got stared at."

Hailey put on a strong face and turned back around and began to glare at the children one at a time until each one of them dropped their eyes, all but Joel. Instead, Joel slowly and deliberately made his way through the group of children until he was directly in front of Hailey, never looking down or away from her eyes.

"Hey girl, were you born in that chair?" Joel blurted out in the most serious voice he could muster.

Hailey had never heard of anything as funny as that in her whole life. She lost her feelings of being afraid and angry and began to laugh hysterically. The other children looked first at Hailey and then at Joel. It must have sounded like a logical question to them, Hailey thought, because they all looked confused. They all acted like they couldn't understand what was so funny.

"Are… you …kidding… or what?" Hailey blurted out between blasts of laughter. "That is so stupid it's funny. What do you think? No wait….were you born with those big clunky shoes on and with that blue hair?'

With that quick comeback, Hailey now had all of Joel's friends laughing at him. Hailey was pretty proud of herself. She had successfully moved the attention of the group from her to the kid who was just trying to stare her down. Even Mrs. Lacey had to cover her mouth with her hand, hiding the smile and giggle that she couldn't keep from coming out.

"We'll, no. That's dumb." Joel answered quietly. "Everybody knows that you aren't born with shoes on," he said, shaking his head up and down while looking over his shoulder at his friends. Hailey could tell that he was trying to act cool and coax someone to agree with him, back him up. Hailey watched as the boy with blue hair searched the faces of his classmates. He seemed to be looking for support, but everyone was still laughing so hard that no one paid any attention to Joel. He was on his own.

Hailey kept going. She had a point to make and she was going to make it. Showing just a bit of regained attitude, she pointed down to the arms of her wheelchair and said, "If everybody knows that people aren't born with shoes on, how come you think I was born in this chair?"

Joel started to answer, but no words came out. He stood there with his mouth wide open, trying to speak. Hailey recognized the frustration and embarrassment on his face. He looked exactly like she felt when people made fun of her. "Well…I don't know…I just thought…," he finally stammered.

Luckily for Joel the first morning bell rang. It was lucky for Mrs. Lacey, too, because it was obvious to Hailey that the teacher wasn't sure how to deal with what was going on between the two of them. "OK, everyone!" She said throwing her hands up in the air, "that's the bell. Let's take this conversation inside to the classroom." She guided her group of third grade students to room number eight.

Once Mrs. Lacey got her students safely inside the classroom and closed the big door with the number eight on it, she turned to the children. She watched as the children milled around the classroom looking for their assigned seats. This took longer than usual or necessary because the children were all talking and pointing at Hailey. Mrs. Lacey walked over to where Hailey was sitting, alone, away from everyone else. She greeted Hailey and guided her to her desk. Hailey rolled up to the last desk in the fifth row. It was a little different than all of the others in the classroom. It was taller than the rest and didn't have a chair.

Mrs. Lacey placed her hand gently on Hailey's shoulder and said, "Hailey, this will be your desk. Since you brought your own chair we found a desk that you and your chair will fit under."

Why is she treating me like a baby Hailey thought to herself while looking up at Mrs. Lacey and faking a smile. "Thanks," she mumbled as she slowly eased up to the desk to see if there was enough room for her knees. She always hated it when she hit her knees on tables and desks that were not tall enough. Fitting nicely under her assigned desk, Hailey found that she had plenty of room for her knees. Hailey looked up again at Mrs. Lacey and nodded her head once to show Mrs. Lacey that the desk would work.

Mrs. Lacey smiled nervously and said, "You will just have to bear with us until we get to know each other better."

"Duh!" Hailey thought to herself. It took a while for Hailey to figure out why her teacher was acting so weird, but now she understood. It was obvious that Mrs. Lacey had never had a disabled student in her class before and was not sure what to do or how to act. Hailey already knew the routine and replied with a quirky look on her face as she contemplated how she was going to help yet, another adult, her teacher, feel more comfortable, "OK, I think I can do that. I'm pretty used to trying new stuff to see if it's going to work."

"Well, good," Mrs. Lacey answered laughing a little.

While Hailey and Mrs. Lacey continued to talk, Hailey watched with one eye and listened with one ear to the rest of the classroom. Robin and Melissa, two of the girls who had been jumping rope before the bell rang, had already found desks across from each other. Shelly, one of the other jump roping girls scanned the classroom. She saw an empty desk in front of Melissa and headed for it.

Shelly had barely sat down before she spun around in her chair and whispered to Robin and Melissa, "Hey, did you see that new girl in a wheelchair? I wonder what's wrong with her."

Robin leaned into the aisle between the rows of desks to answer. "I don't know. I guess she can't walk or something."

Shelly flipped back around to check out her desk. Melissa tapped her on the back and continued, "I bet she can't hear or talk either. My mom says that people like that are retarded. She says that people like that are just dumb and can't learn anything."

Hailey could feel her ears turn red as she caught little bits of the conversations. They always turned red when she got mad. She was glad that her hair was covering them so no one could see.

Then Hailey saw Simon, who was holding up his cast as he walked past the three girls. Hailey could tell that he was trying to hold it up, probably so he wouldn't hit anything, she thought. She secretly hoped that he would bonk the girl named Melissa on the head when he stopped to listen to them talk. Then she heard him say, "Yeah, that's what I heard too, but how come she's in school if she's that way? I mean, she must not be if she is at school."

"Well …, I don't know. That's just what my mom says." Melissa defended herself and shrugged her shoulders at the same time.

Simon continued down the rows until he reached a desk in the front of the classroom. His friends were already there having a pretend sword fight. They were making a real racket, bumping into desks and shouting at each other. The boys were so loud that it caused Hailey and Mrs. Lacey to stop talking and look to see where all the noise was coming from. Hailey looked back at Mrs. Lacey and saw that she had a scowl on her face and her hands on her hips. "Busted." Hailey whispered to herself.

"Class!" Mrs. Lacey yelled, "we need to turn the volume way down here. We need to use our quiet inside voices and not our loud outside ones. Everyone find a seat and settle down." She walked up to her big desk at the front of the room and glanced over at Hailey, who was sitting very quietly and looking very serious. When the room finally got silent and her students were all looking up at her, Mrs. Lacey began her first day of class speech.

"Now let's get our first day of school started," Mrs. Lacey began. "Most of you know me because you were at this school last year. But, if you don't, my name is Mrs. Lacey."

With no warning Blake jumped up out of his seat and hollered, "Hey, Mrs. Lacey, what's the matter with that girl?"

Hailey looked back and forth from Blake to Mrs. Lacey. Hailey could tell that Mrs. Lacey was shocked and surprised by Blake's outburst. She acted like she had not expected it and was not sure how to handle it. Hailey almost jumped out of her wheelchair when Mrs. Lacey seemed to shout out the first thing that came to her mind. "Blake, hush!!! We can't get anything started if you are talking. That goes for all of you. I should be the only one talking right now. So when you are all quiet I'll start again." Mrs. Lacey looked at the notes on her desk while she waited for the class to settle down. The students looked sheepish and a little uncomfortable as they whispered to each other for a few seconds. Then they all turned to face the front of the classroom and their teacher.

Hailey saw Mrs. Lacey shoot her a sideways glance, probably to see how she was reacting to Blake's question she guessed. Hailey was sitting quietly and motionless. She was staring at the back of the head of the person seated in front of her. Hailey pretended to be made of stone and did not even blink. Hailey was used to this kind of question, but it still upset her and made her mad. People like Blake were always asking questions about her and trying to make her feel different from the rest of the world. It was something she expected. It was something her mother had prepared her for, too, and Hailey was sure that she could prove to her new classmates that she was just like them. So she sat and waited patiently for her chance to show them that she belonged.

Finally the class was quiet enough for Mrs. Lacey to continue, and she began her speech again. "Does anyone know how we start each day?" she asked.

Robin, raising her hand and waving it wildly in the air, was barely able to stay in her seat calling out, "I do. I do, Mrs. Lacey!"

Smiling, Mrs. Lacey pointed to Robin for her answer. Robin jumped up out of her chair and answered. "We say the 'Pledge of 'llegiance."

"That is absolutely right, Robin," Mrs. Lacey replied. "So everyone please *quietly* stand up, face the flag, put your right hand over your heart, and we will say the 'Pledge of Allegiance.'"

There was a swirl of excitement as the children began the first day of their new classroom routine. As the class began to push back their chairs and jump to their feet, Hailey saw Mrs. Lacey shake her head back and forth. The chairs were scraping along the floor, the children were again talking and laughing, and the boys were pretending to have boxing matches. Hailey bet that she knew what Mrs. Lacey was thinking and silently agreed. "Yep, they're gonna need to practice doing it quietly, a whole lot of practice." The good part was that they had all forgotten about her, the new girl, at the last desk in the fifth row. Once again Mrs. Lacey looked over at Hailey before she addressed the rest of the class. She saw that Hailey sat unwaveringly with her hand over her heart, ready to begin. Returning her attention to the now semi-organized class, Mrs. Lacey asked, "Are we ready?"

All of the children stopped what they were doing and looked up and answered as one voice. "Yes."

"All right then, Mrs. Lacey continued, "let's begin." Mrs. Lacey put her hand over her heart and lead the class in the 'Pledge of Allegiance.' After she got them going Mrs. Lacey let the class recite the Pledge on their own as she listened.

> "I pledge 'llegiance to the flag of the United
> States of America, To the 'public for which
> it stands, one nation, under God, 'invisible
> with liberty and justice for all."

As the class finished the Pledge of Allegiance and took their seats, Mrs. Lacey smiled and said, "Well, that was very good. We might need a small bit of practice though."

Before Mrs. Lacey had a chance to take a breath and move on to the next activity of the day, Joel jumped up out of his seat again and pointed at Hailey and screamed, "Mrs. Lacey, Mrs. Lacey, the new girl didn't stand up. How come she didn't stand up? You're supposed to stand up."

By the look on Mrs. Lacey's face, Hailey could tell that she had been caught off guard again, only this time by Joel. Hailey wasn't surprised and had sort of expected the kids to be curious about her and her wheelchair, but she didn't think they would have been so vocal about it. Usually people didn't say anything to her or about her when she was around. Most of the time people would wait until she was gone or at least far enough away that she couldn't hear them. That's when they would stare or sneak looks at her just like Mrs. Lacey was doing now. Hailey felt sorry for Mrs. Lacey when she noticed that she was shooting an embarrassed and apologetic glance in her direction. "Gosh," thought Hailey, "how can I show her I'm okay with that dweeby blue-haired boy's question? This should work," she answered herself, and with that Hailey sat with one elbow resting on her desk twisting her index finger in circles by the side of her head. Hailey's reaction gave Mrs. Lacey the cue to go on. Mrs. Lacey rested her hands on her hips and sternly scolded Joel.

"Joel, please sit down and listen! You can't learn anything if you don't listen."

While the class began to settle and quiet down, Mrs. Lacey gave Hailey a second quick look before she continued. "Good morning everyone," she said. "I have an idea. Since you all seem to want to talk, let's learn and talk at the same time. I want you to listen to my instructions and then think very carefully about what you are going to say. I have already introduced myself to you. Now it is your turn to introduce yourselves and share one thing that is special about you or that you think is important for us to know about you. Blake, why don't you start?"

Blake sat for a moment and seemed to be thinking about what he wanted to say. "I know that most everyone knows my name, well maybe not the new girl," he started and then stopped again. "Okay, so it's kind of hard to decide what to tell you guys what's special or important about me on account of I never thought about it. Let me think," Blake added. Hailey watched Blake as he sat and then slowly slid out of his chair and stand beside his desk. Softly Blake began, "Okay, my name is Blake and I'm the tallest boy in the third grade."

Before Blake had even sat down at his desk, Joel jumped up and blasted out his speech. "Hi, my name is Joel, and I know just about everything there is to know about cars." Then with an exaggerated bow Joel sat down and immediately began to turn in all directions to survey the class for their reaction. Joel was looking all proud of himself when he finally sat down at his desk, facing forward with his hands folded on his desktop while Melissa stood waiting to begin her introduction.

"My name is Melissa," she said pointing to her shirt, "and I got to go to Disneyland this summer."

Then Rita leapt up and stated that her name was Rita and that she had a twin brother named Simon, and then sat back down just as fast. "Hey, I was gonna use that one!" Simon raised his hand and declared without bothering to stand up. Rita twisted around in her chair and stuck her tongue out at her brother and laughed. Hailey could tell by the look on his face that it took all the control Simon had not to smack Rita for stealing what was special about him, even though she was part of why he was special, a twin.

The whole class began to laugh at Simon. Hailey didn't know that most of her new classmates had known both Rita and Simon since kindergarten and knew that they were always trying to out-do each other, but she laughed anyway. The twins kept the children entertained most of the time with their competitions and their need to be first or best at everything.

Mrs. Lacey appeared to have been startled by the confrontation and quickly jumped in to defuse the argument between brother and sister. "That's O.K. Simon. You can both use the same one."

Simon stayed seated for several seconds acting like he was pouting and hurt. Then, only standing halfway out of his chair, Simon hurried through his version of Rita's speech . "Well, like Rita said, my name is Simon and I have a twin sister, Rita."

The remaining introductions went smoothly. There was no more laughing or hitting or making fun. Simon and Rita had made the classroom feel more comfortable. Hailey was beginning to feel more at ease in her new surroundings, especially since the children in her new class were paying more attention to Simon and Rita than to her and her wheelchair. She wondered if Mrs. Lacey noticed it too, that Simon and Rita's fight had made it easier for the rest of the class to speak in front of each other, had made the classroom more comfortable. Hailey found that she felt calm and confident enough to lean forward in her chair with her elbows on her desk and rest her chin on her hands to listen to the remaining members of the class introduce themselves.

Hailey was pretty good at remembering names so she paid more attention to the other things her classmates said, the things they thought were important to know. While she listened, she practiced in her head what she was going to share with the class. It wasn't too long before there were only two more girls left ahead of Hailey to speak.

Robin popped up from her desk and giggled. "Hi, you guys all know that my name is Robin, but did you know that my mom works at this school? She's a teacher like Mrs. Lacey." Robin giggled again and plopped back down in her seat as fast as she rose up out of it.

Hailey watched as the last girl slid out of her desk and stood for a minute. Then she slowly began, "My name is Michelle, but people call me Shelly because it's easier. I guess what's special about me is that I am really good at math. I know it's weird for a girl to like math, but I do."

Hailey swallowed hard and smiled when she realized that it was her turn to speak. She scanned the faces of her new classmates while the whole class, including Mrs. Lacey, watched and waited for Hailey to introduce herself. Hailey could tell that Mrs. Lacey was going to try and help her, talk for her, probably introduce her to the class like she was nervous or something, but before Mrs. Lacey could say anything Hailey swiftly raised her head off of her hands, dropping her arms down on her desk and said, "Hi! I guess I'm the newest girl in this whole school. My name is Hailey, and I am learning how to sew on a sewing machine. My grandma is teaching me how."

Mrs. Lacey had been sitting on the edge of her big wooden desk at the front of the room during the introductions. When Hailey had finished introducing herself to the class, Mrs. Lacey stood up and took a deep breath as she walked around to sit in her chair. Hailey sensed a feeling of relief in her voice when she heard Mrs. Lacey say "Well, that went well." When she reached her chair, Mrs. Lacey sat down and praised the class for the wonderful job they had done. "Very good, I am so very pleased with how well you did. What magnificent speakers we have in this class. I am very glad to meet all of you."

"Okay, let's move on," continued Mrs. Lacey. "I really had not planned on starting class this way. Usually on the first day of school my students are pretty quiet and shy, but none of you seem to have that problem. In fact," she added with a laugh, "it looks like you all have ideas of your own."

Simon, who was sitting in the front row, quietly asked, "What do you mean, Mrs. Lacey?"

Hailey watched as Mrs. Lacey fumbled, trying to gather her words to explain and then look to the back of the room where she sat. Hailey realized what was coming and groaned. She knew that Mrs. Lacey was going to end her next sentence with the word *disability.*

"Are you all right, Hailey?" Mrs. Lacey questioned after hearing the noise.

Hailey smiled and shook her head up and down. "Yeah, I mean yes, I'm okay."

Mrs. Lacey returned to answering Simon's question just as Joel leaned forward on his desk and raised his hand again, waving it over the top of his head. Hailey was aware that Mrs. Lacey was purposely ignoring Joel's attempt to get her attention as she began to answer Simon's question. "I don't think it's gonna work, Mrs. Lacey," Hailey silently mouthed.

"What I mean, Simon…" Mrs. Lacey was unable to finish before Joel blurted out, "Mrs. Lacey, Mrs. Lacey."

Mrs. Lacey sprang to her feet squelching Joel's outburst. "No. Joel. No more questions. I want to talk about something else right now. You need to listen now and not talk."

Joel could not be stopped. He pointed at Hailey and proceeded with his investigation, "…but how come she didn't say that her wheelchair made her special?"

"Well Joel," Mrs. Lacey stated, "maybe that's because Hailey doesn't think that her wheelchair makes her special."

Joel, looked and acted like he still did not really understand, scratching his head in a frustrating way. "But I don't get it," he tried to add, "how come a wheelchair doesn't make some one special or at least different?"

"Well Joel, if you will do as I ask and sit down and listen maybe you will get it," Mrs. Lacey repeated.

Hailey figured that Joel didn't know what other questions to ask so that he could understand, when she heard him utter, "oh, Okay," and sit down without another word.

    Hailey thought that Mrs. Lacey was kind of impatient in her response, but decided it was probably the only way she knew of to get Joel back on track. It may have sounded grouchy, but it worked. Now she had Joel and the rest of the class under control and their attention. Mrs. Lacey took a deep breath and blew it out. Then she looked around the room and without hesitation plunged right into her speech. "We need to talk about some things that are very important. First of all, listening to some of you this morning I have heard some words that are not very nice and maybe even hurtful." Mrs. Lacey turned and faced the whiteboard. She picked up a bright red pen and wrote two words, "dumb" and "retarded." Mrs. Lacey continued speaking while she placed the cap back on the pen and set it on the ledge of the whiteboard. She pointed to the words, "We won't be using these kinds of words from now on. Girls, you know who you are."

Shelly, Robin and Melissa looked at each other as they slapped their hands over their mouths. The girls looked mortified by being singled out, and each girl turned a different shade of red. "Man," Hailey thought, "if she had wanted to make a point and embarrass those girls, she sure got the job done."

Mrs. Lacey smiled at the girls and picked up where she had left off. "That said, today we are going to learn another word, a very important word."

Mrs. Lacey turned to face the whiteboard again. She chose a different colored pen, a blue one this time and wrote in big, block letters, DISABILITY.

She slowly set the pen down and turned back around. Mrs. Lacey stood quietly for a few minutes and watched. Hailey assumed that she was trying to give the children time to look at the word and try to figure out what it was and what it meant. Then she asked, "Can anyone tell me what this word is? Anyone besides Hailey, I know she knows what it is and what it means. That might give the rest of you a hint."

Hailey was also looking at the faces of her new classmates, some were really funny. She wanted to laugh at them and say "Duh, you guys!" but she didn't because she didn't want to be mean or hurt anyone's feelings. She knew what that was like, and she didn't like it. Instead, she watched as several children tried to say the word softly to themselves. Others shrugged their shoulders. Some wagged their heads. A few just turned and stared at Hailey again.

Pointing to each syllable, Mrs. Lacey pronounces the word. "Dis a bil i ty." Then she said the word with all of the syllables together. "Disability. Let's all say it together."

All of the children chimed in, "Disability."

"Does anyone know what this word means?" asked Mrs. Lacey.

Once again all of the children in the class shook their heads back and forth. "No, Nope, Nah-Ah," was what they all answered, all except Hailey. She was bobbing her head up and down and answering the question in her head, "Yeah, of course I know."

It was now obvious to Hailey that Mrs. Lacey was finally on a roll. She had the class's attention, they were quiet, and they seemed to be thinking. But it didn't last too long because before she could continue, Joel began frantically waving his hand in the air over his blue hair for the umpteenth time. "But Mrs. Lacey," he started, "what does that have to do with the new girl? I mean, what's her name? Oh, yeah, Hailey. What's the matter with her?"

"Joel," Mrs. Lacey pleaded, "listen to me for a minute. I really did have a plan for what we were going to do and talk about, but your interruptions aren't helping. What I intended to do was talk about a word, a word that is going to be new for most of you. I wanted you to learn the definition."

"Okay," Joel returned, "but"

"No, let me finish," Mrs. Lacey continued as she began to write on the whiteboard and ramrod through the speech she had practiced. "Look, the main part of the word, or root word, is <u>ability</u>. That part means having the power to do something. The first part of the word, <u>dis</u>, which is called a prefix, means not. When the two parts are put together, the meaning of the root word changes."

"Like when we say 'don't dis me' when we mean don't disrespect me," Hailey piped up, "because respect is a good thing, but dis-ing is a bad thing."

"Exactly, Hailey!" Mrs. Lacey answered. "Thank you."

"Oh great," Hailey mused as the whole class turned to gawk at her. "So much for being incognito. Me and my big mouth."

"Hailey, would you mind if I used you as an example to help me explain?" Mrs. Lacey asked.

"I guess not," Hailey answered and settled back in her chair to listen.

"Well," Mrs. Lacey chirped with renewed enthusiasm, "as you have all noticed, Hailey uses a wheelchair. She uses the wheelchair because she has a disability. Her disability is that she can't walk by herself. But Hailey isn't all that different from you and me." Mrs. Lacey pointed at her feet. "You see, I have always had very big feet, and I sometimes trip over them myself. That is my disability. We all have some type of disability. Some of us have disabilities that we can see and some of us have disabilities that we can't see." She paused for a moment and glanced around the classroom. The children all looked more confused than ever to Hailey. How is Mrs. Lacey going to help them understand Hailey wondered? So she watched for several seconds as Mrs. Lacey studied her students and came up with a new strategy. "Okay," she started again, "we all know that Robin wears glasses to help her see better, right?"

The children hesitated then look at each other and nodded their heads in agreement. Hesitantly and a little unsure they answer.
"Yeah," they all answered.

"Sure," Joel added, "of course we all know that Robin wears glasses, but I still don't know what that has to do with the new girl and somebody's big feet."

"Great!" Mrs. Lacey declared with excitement and once again ignoring Joel's uncertainty. "Well that is Robin's disability. Let's take someone else. How about Blake? We have all seen that Blake wears hearing aids. Blake's disability is that he isn't able to hear as well as the rest of us. His hearing aids helps him hear better."

Joel reacted with surprise. "Huh?" He popped out of his seat with his hands on the top of his head, confessing, "Oh, wow, yeah. I forgot all about that. Me and Blake have been friends like forever and he has always had hearing aids. I guess I just got used to him having them. That is kinda weird, but cool, too."

"That's right, Joel." Mrs. Lacey agreed. "That is cool. I think what happens is that once you get to know someone, you forget that they have a disability or that they need help in some way. And remember how Shelly always complains that she is too short to reach the shelf with the crayons? That is her disability, being short."

Most of the children in the class grinned and looked at Shelly while they bobbed their heads up and down in agreement. "Sure, we help her get stuff down from the tall shelves all the time," Blake said. "It really makes her mad that she can't reach things by herself. We don't mind helping her though. Most of the time we don't even think about it; we just do it."

Hailey couldn't help but notice that Shelly sat with her arms crossed looking surprised and annoyed at the same time. Hailey didn't blame her either. It wasn't exactly like Mrs. Lacey was making fun of Shelly or anything; it was more like Mrs. Lacey was focusing on only one part of Shelly, the part that made her most different than everyone else. People did that to Hailey all the time. They just saw her wheelchair and not her. Then just as Mrs. Lacey was about to respond to Blake's observation, Hailey caught Shelly peering over her shoulder to sneak a quick look to the back of the room where she was sitting. "Gosh," Shelly stammered, "I bet the new girl feels exactly the same way I do. I bet she gets mad when people talk about and make fun of her, too. I hate being short, I hate being reminded that I'm short and most of all, I hate being made fun of because I'm short."

Mrs. Lacey chuckled and replied to both Shelly and Blake. "Hmmm, pretty interesting isn't it? I think you both are absolutely right, though. All of you are very good about helping each other, just like when you help Melissa when she gets her letters mixed up. You help her sort them out and remember which one is which. And it is very unkind to make fun and call people names. It makes them feel bad."

Mrs. Lacey paused to let the children take in what had just been said. Her eyes skimmed and studied the faces of the children in the classroom. One by one each third grade student shows a flicker of understanding. Hailey could see that they were beginning to grasp the definition of the word disability and the lesson that came with knowing what the word really means.

All of a sudden Rita threw her hand in the air. Without being called on she asked and answered her own question. "Mrs. Lacey, you mean that a disability is something that doesn't work exactly right?"

Before Mrs. Lacey could get a word out, Robin added, "Or the way it is supposed too...like your feet. I mean you said you trip because your feet are too big, right? Well, like doesn't that mean that they don't work the way they are supposed to? Sweet! I so get it now!"

Hailey heard Mrs. Lacey whisper "Score," under her breath. She looked as if could hardly contain her excitement. "Yes!" Mrs. Lacey blurted out. "That is precisely right. Very good Rita and Robin, you see, anyone can have a disability, but it doesn't really make them any different than you and me. There are all kinds of disabilities. Some you can see and some you can't see. In fact, I would even say that everyone has some kind of disability."

"That's 'cause nobody's perfect, huh?" Rita added. "I know 'cause I have a brother, Simon," she threw in with a giggle.

At the sound of his name being mentioned, Simon flipped around in his chair and made a face at his sister. "Darn," Simon growled. "I wish I had thought of that," he announced to the class, "but Rita has always been a tiny smidgen smarter than me, probably because she's three and a half minutes older than I am. She's not a lot smarter," he added holding up his thumb and forefinger," just a tad, ya know, just enough that she catches me off guard and can poke fun at me." Hailey catch sight of a funny look moving across Simon's face. "I'm used to it though, and it always gives me a reason to punch her." The whole class, even Rita laughed as Simon began to shadow box.

"That is exactly right, Rita. No one is perfect." Mrs. Lacey answered trying to stifle a laugh and ignore Simon.

Hailey shook her head up and down in approval, but she was growing impatient of sitting in the background. She had sat listening to the whole 'being disabled thing' long enough. She wanted to be part of the conversation. "La, la, la," she sang to herself swinging her head from side to side. "I think the class pretty much gets the meaning of the word disability, Mrs. Lacey. Remember, they even used examples. Can we like, please talk about something else?" Hailey wished quietly to herself. Then Hailey had an idea. She sat up taller in her wheelchair, bit her lower lip, and raised her hand.

"Yes, Hailey," Mrs. Lacey said.

"And blue is definitely not the perfect color for hair," she answered, throwing a look and big toothy grin at Joel.

"Good one, Hailey," Melissa called out.

"Hey!" Joel yelled as he spun around in his seat to look at Hailey. The whole class began to laugh, even Joel. "The act performed was beyond my control," he continued. "I told you guys that my big brother did it."

Luckily, and before Mrs. Lacey had a chance to intervene, Joel was saved from any further humiliation by the ringing of a bell. On cue, Mrs. Lacey clapped her hands together. "That bell means that it's time for recess, she announced.

"Finally," Hailey murmured, "recess is the perfect time to change the subject and maybe make some new friends." Maybe Mrs. Lacey's lesson helped, Hailey admitted to herself. Maybe this morning's discussion had made a difference in the attitude of the kids in the class and how they would act toward her now. She was hoping that recess was going to be way different than when she first arrived at school today.

There did seem to be a problem though. Well, not really a problem, but something odd and out of the ordinary. As Hailey began to make her way closer to the door, she realized that the children in the class were milling around their desks', reluctant to go outside. Being disabled was a non-issue as far as she was concerned. If they wanted to be all weird about it, that was their business. Hailey knew how to stand up for herself and meet head-on any question or situation that the kids in her new class could throw at her. She really wanted to get to know more about her classmates, especially that blue-haired boy. He was kind of funny and maybe even a little cute, but it didn't look like that was happening.

"What's the deal," Hailey heard Mrs. Lacey ask, "What seems to be the problem here? Let's go, everyone outside." But no one moved except Mrs. Lacey who walked to the center of the room. "Is this a hint as to how this year is going to go?" she asked, "You appear to have an agenda of your own. Anyone want to fill me in?"

After several seconds, Melissa marched up to Mrs. Lacey and boldly asked, "Do we have to go outside? We all want to stay in and talk to Hailey and stuff?"

"Yeah!" They all chimed in nodding their heads in support of the idea.

"That would be really awesome!" Robin excitedly added while pushing her glasses up higher on her nose with her index finger.

"That sounds like a wonderful idea to me. What do you think Hailey? Are you up for that?" Mrs. Lacey asked. "It's up to you."

"Sure, I guess that's okay with me," Hailey answered as she flipped her wheelchair around to face the rest of the children.

"All right then." Mrs. Lacey continued, "You can stay in and get to know each other." Then turning and heading for her desk, she added, "If anyone needs anything, I'll be at my desk."

All of the children opted to stay in the classroom during this recess instead of going outside to the playground, even the boys. There would be plenty of time to play basketball and jump rope and jacks and other games later. Hailey maneuvered herself between and around the rows of desks to an open space in the classroom. The whole class gathered around Hailey and, all at once, started introducing themselves. They couldn't seem to get close enough to her and tried to push each other out of the way, but soon settled down. Hailey giggled as they began to shoot questions at her faster than she could possibly answer them. Joel, the blue-haired boy, elbowed his way to the front of the crowd and shouted, "Hey, how fast can you go in that thing?"

Rita stepped up, pulling at her red hair. "Look! I have a disability, too. We didn't talk about it in class, but my hair is way too curly. It never works right. I really wish it was straight. Then I could get it to do what I wanted it to."

Simon, Rita's twin brother pushed her out of the way. He held up his casted arm in Rita's face and then pointed at it. "No, you look! I have a real disability. Not a made up one like yours." He stopped for a second to think and then wondered out loud. "Hey, I have freckles, too. They make me and Rita different than you guys," he said pointing at his friends. "Is that a disability?"

Unsure, they all shrugged their shoulders. "I don't think so," Hailey answered with a snort. Freckles don't *dooo* anything. They're just kind of there."

Blake and another boy walked around to the back of the wheelchair, looking, pointing and touching everything. "Whoa, check this out! It has two batteries, like car batteries," exclaimed Blake. "I bet it's got tons of power." After examining the back of the chair more closely, he also reported to another classmate that Hailey had a super place to carry a backpack. "Yeah, check it out dude! How lucky is she? She doesn't have to carry a thousand pound bag on her back like we do. Her chair does it for her. Too cool."

Hailey had her hands full attempting to make sure that Blake didn't touch or unplug anything, while at the same time carrying on a conversation with the girls in the class. Joel surprised the whole group by bumping Simon out of his way and standing directly in front of Hailey. He cleared his throat loudly to gain her attention. "Hi, Hailey, he said. "I'm Joel. Can I drive your chair?"

Hailey decided to pretend to ignore Joel and looked the other way, rolling her eyes. Robin, Shelly, Melissa, Rita, and the rest of the girls all started to laugh and ignored Joel, too. He started to say something else, but the girls all threw their hands up in front of him. "We're talking here, man. Quit interrupting and being so rude!" Melissa spouted.

"Yeah, Joel!" all the girls added.

"Okay, okay," Joel answered back. "But can we talk after, Hailey?"

Hailey felt a little sorry for Joel. She knew what it felt like to be ignored, and she felt sort of bad that she had made fun of him. "Sure," She said with a smile. "And, yes, you can drive my chair. Everyone always asks me that. But later, though."

"Sweet!" Joel shouted, pumping his arm as he leaned to look at what the other boys were inspecting on the back of the chair.

"Where were we?" Robin questioned. "Oh, right. Hailey, I really love your sweater. It's really pretty."

"Thanks. I got it at Mervyn's. It was on sale," Hailey replied, rubbing the fuzzy sleeve of her purple sweater. "You can borrow it sometime if you want."

"So, hey, where do you live, anyway?" Shelly piped up. "Can we come over after school?" she continued as she pointed to several of the girls in the group.

Hailey beamed from ear to ear. "I live on Locust Avenue, around the corner from the park. That would be great but probably not today 'cause I have to clean my room first. My mom won't let me have company if my room is all messy."

"Yeah, I know what you mean, mine, too." Rita agreed. "Moms are weird that way. I have an idea. How about we give each other our phone numbers and E-mail addresses? That way we can ask if we can maybe hangout tomorrow after school and then set it up. I guess that means we all have to clean our rooms before we do anything, huh?"

Melissa ripped a piece of paper out of her binder and started the list of names, numbers and addresses. Just as the last girl added her information to the list the bell rang for the end of recess.

"We finished just in time," Hailey noted and headed back to her desk. The rest of the class did the same. "Yep, I'm going to like my school," she spoke softly to herself.

Mrs. Lacey caught the tail end of Blake and Joel's conversation as they returned to their desks. "I wonder what tomorrow's word is gonna be." Blake asked.

Joel answered with confidence, "Yeah, the one today was way too easy."

THE END

Were You Born In That Chair?

Note to parents and teachers: Please feel free to photo-copy the following script and outline-drawings. The drawings should be copied onto heavy cardstock if possible. Have your children cut out the figures and color them before gluing them to popsicle sticks.

Were You Born in That Chair?
Play

Lights come up-center stage

SCENE I: *Children begin to gather on the school yard in front of the classroom. Small groups of children who know each other begin to from and get reacquainted, laughing and shouting, as the teacher looks on from the door of classroom number eight. Hailey sits at the edge of the playground. She stays there for a while and watches. Then she slowly begins to make her way across the playground to room number eight.*

BLAKE: *(running toward a redheaded, freckled faced boy named Simon from stage left)* Hey dude, how'd you break your arm? Are you in Mrs. Lacey's class?

SIMON: Yeah, are you? I was hoping ya would be 'cause you have the best Pokemon cards of everybody. Besides that, I don't know if I'll know anybody else, and we can hang out together.

BLAKE: Yeah, that will be cool, but how did you break your arm?

SIMON: Well, we got a pool this summer, so I spent a lot of time swimming and Stuff until Rita dared me to do a double back flip off the diving board, and I broke my arm doing it.

BLAKE: How do you do stuff like tie your shoes if you can't use your arm?

SIMON: That's easy. Me and my dad went to the shoe store and bought some with Velcro, ya know, that stuff that sticks to itself, so I don't have'ta tie 'em. But my mom has'ta help me comb my hair, and I gotta wear T-shirts 'cause I can't do the buttons.

BLAKE: That must really suck.

SIMON: Naw. It's not so bad. You kinda get use to it. Hey, look, there's Joel!
(Simon and Blake run toward Joel, past two girls playing jacks near the classroom door. They notice and point to Joel's new hairstyle and color.)

BLAKE: Hey Joel, your mom let you dye your hair blue? My mom would never let me do that.

JOEL: Well, my mom didn't really let me do it. She wasn't home and my big brother wanted to test it on me before he did his ... I heard they were gonna get new basketballs this year. Let's go check it out.

(Boys exit right cutting through a dodge ball game, running past a group of girls playing jump rope.)

KIDS PLAYING DODGEBALL: Hey, you guys, get out of the way! Go around!

GIRLS PLAYING JUMP ROPE: *(as Rita jumps)*...blue Bells, cockle shells, easy, ivy over Hots! 1, 2, 3, 4, 5, 6

SHELLY: You missed! It's Robin's turn

ROBIN: *(walking toward Melissa's end of the rope, and taking off her glasses, she hands them to Melissa.)* Would you hold these for me so I don't drop and break them or something?

MELISSA: Yeah, I'll put them here in my pocket.

ROBIN: *(turning toward Shelly)* Hey, Shelly, let's do twenty-four robbers.

SHELLY: Sure. OK. You start and then I'll be the robbers and jump in.

ROBIN: Ready?

Girls start to sing as Robin begins to jump.

GIRLS: Not last night, but the night before, twenty-four robbers came knockin' at my door. As I ran out... *(Robin jumps out and Shelly jumps in)* they came in... *(girls voices fade into background)*

(From stage right the boys come running back from checking out the balls past the girls jumping rope. The boys begin to play a mock game of basketball. Blake runs backwards, blocking Simon, who is pretending to dribble the ball with his good arm, Joel follows, pretending to block for him, all the time yelling basketball terms. Blake backs into the wheelchair, looses his balance and the ball, and falls down.)

BLAKE: *(looks up from the ground at the person who he believes ran into him)* Hey, get out of the way! Watch where you're going. We're trying to play basketball. You gotta...OHHHHH

(Blake stands up and the rest of the boys back up as they stare at Hailey, the girl in the wheelchair. All the children notice the commotion and look in that direction. They also stare at Hailey.)

BLAKE: *(stepping forward)* Are you in the right school? I haven't seen you here before, and I know most everybody. We don't have kids like you at this school. What's the matter with you anyway? How come you are in that thing? Is it like a golf cart or scooter or something?

Were You Born In That Chair?

HAILEY: *(looking defiant)* No, it's not a scooter or something. It's a wheelchair.

(Mrs. Lacey hurries nervously out of the classroom to greet Hailey and intervene in the coming conflict.)

MRS. LACEY: You must be Hailey. I'm so pleased to finally meet you. My name is Mrs. Lacey, and I'm going to be your teacher this year.

HAILEY: *(feeling apprehensive looks around)* Hello.

(The other children begin to migrate in the direction of Mrs. Lacey and Hailey. They form a semi-circle around the two of them, speechless, but still staring.)

HAILEY: *(a little afraid, but now also angry looks around and then back to Mrs. Lacey)* Why do people have to do that, stare I mean? How come they just cant's see me and that I'm pretty much like everyone else. I bet they wouldn't like it if they got stared at.

(Hailey puts on a strong face, turns and begins to glare at the children, one at a time, until they drop their eyes, all but Joel. Joel slowly and deliberately makes his way through the group and stops directly in front of Hailey, never removing his eyes from hers. Mrs. Lacey watches with anticipation, unsure of what to do.)

JOEL: *(very seriously)* Hey girl, were you born in that chair?

HAILEY: *(begins to laugh hysterically. The other children look confused.)* Are you kidding or what? That is so stupid it's funny. What do you think? No, wait...were you born with those big clunky shoes on and with that blue hair?

(All of the children explode into laughter. Even Mrs. Lacey tries to hide a smile behind her hands.)

JOEL: Well, no. That's dumb. Everybody knows that you aren't born with shoes on.

(Joel surveys the faces of his friends, looking for support, shaking his head up and down.)

HAILEY: If everybody knows that people aren't born with shoes on, then how come you think I was born in this chair...*(points to arm of the wheelchair)* If that isn't dumb, I don't know what is.

JOEL: Well...I don't know, I just thought...

(The bell rings.)

MRS. LACEY: OK, everyone, that's the bell. Let's take this conversation inside the classroom.

FADE TO BLACK.

Lights come up in the interior of a classroom

SCENE II: *Children are milling around the classroom looking for their assigned seats, talking and pointing at Hailey,*
Mrs. Lacey guides Hailey to her desk. Hailey rolls up to the last desk in the fifth row. The desk is taller than the rest and doesn't have a chair.

MRS. LACEY: Hailey, this will be your desk. Since you brought your own chair, We found a desk that we hope you will fit under. You'll just have to bear with us until we get to know each other better.

HAILEY: *(smiles at Mrs. Lacey)* OK, I think I can do that. I'm pretty used to trying new stuff to see if it is gonna work.

MRS. LACEY: *(Smiling back at Hailey)* Well, good. That should make it easier for us to work together.

(Mrs. Lacey and Hailey's voices fade into the background. The lights fade out on the two of them and fade in on the group of girls in the classroom. Finding a desk with her name on it, near where Robin and Melissa are sitting, she sits down and turns to talk to them.)

SHELLY: Did you see that girl? She's in a wheelchair. I wonder what's wrong with her. I never knew anyone in a wheelchair before, have you guys?

(Both girls shake their heads.)

ROBIN: *(leaning into the aisle)* I don't know. I guess she can't walk or something.

MELISSA: Duh! *(tapping Shelly on the back)* I bet she can't hear or talk either. My mom says that people like that are retarded ya know. She says that people like that are just dumb and can't learn nothin.

SIMON: *(walking past the girls to a desk in the front of the room holding up his casted arm)* Yeah, that's what I heard, too. But how come she's in school if she's that way? I mean, she must not be dumb if she is at school.

MELISSA: Well..., I don't know. That's just what my mom says.

(Lights come up on the whole stage. The other boys are playing around, pretending to sword fight, making a lot of noise. The girls laugh loudly. Mrs. Lacey turns away from Hailey to face the rest of the class. She has a scowl on her face and her hands on her hips.)

MRS. LACEY: Class! We need to turn the volume way down here and use our inside voices, not our outside ones. *(Mrs. Lacey pauses and waits for the children to find their seats and quiet down. She moves to the front of the classroom where her big desk is.*

Were You Born In That Chair?

She looks down at her notes as she waits. When the children are settled, she continues.)
Now, let's get our first day of class started. Most of you know me because you were at this school last year, but if you don't, my name is Mrs. Lacey

BLAKE: (excitedly) Hey, Mrs. Lacey, what's the matter with that girl!

MRS. LACEY: Blake!!! Hush!!! We can't get anything started if you are talking. That goes for all of you. I should be the only one talking right now. So when you are quiet, I'll start.

(Mrs. Lacey looks back down at her notes as she waits for the class to settle down again. The students look around at each other for a few seconds, some whisper and then begin to face the front of the class room. Hailey sits quietly and motionless staring at the back of the head seated in front of her.)

MRS. LACEY: Does anyone know how we start each day?

ROBIN: *(raising her hand wildly)* I do! I do Mrs. Lacey. We say the Pledge of 'llegiance.

MRS. LACEY: That's right Robin. So, everyone stand up, face the flag, put your hand over your heart, and we will say the Pledge of Allegiance.

ALL OF THE CHILDRN: (following Mrs. Lacey's instructions) I pledge 'llegiance to the flag of the United States of America, to the 'public for which it stands, one nation under God, invisible, with liberty and justice for all.

JOEL: (pointing) Mrs. Lacey, the new girl didn't stand up. How come she didn't stand up? You're suppose to stand up.

MRS. LACEY: *(a bit shocked and unnerved)* Joel, please sit down and listen! You can't learn if you don't listen. *(The class is now suddenly quiet, she begins again.)* Good morning everyone. I have introduced myself to you already. Now it's your turn to introduce yourselves to each other and tell us something About yourselves, something that makes you different or maybe something that is special about you. Blake, why don't you start.

(Each child stands up and introduces themselves.)

BLAKE: OK, well my name is Blake, and I'm the tallest boy in first grade.

JOEL: My name is Joel, and I know just about everything there is to know about cars.

MELISSA: My name is Melissa and I gotta go to Disneyland this summer.

RITA: My name is Rita, and I have a twin brother, Simon. He's in this class, too.

SIMON: Hey, I was gonna use that one!

MRS. LACEY: That's OK Simon. You can both use the same one.

SIMON: Well, then...my name is Simon and have a twin sister named Rita.
(*Simon sticks his tongue out at Rita.*)

ROBIN: Hi, my name is Robin, and my mom works at this school. She's a teacher at this school, too, just like Mrs. Lacey.

SHELLY: My name is Shelly and I am really good with numbers, ya know adding and subtracting, and like that. (*Everyone turns around in their chairs to look at the new girl.*)

HAILEY: My name is Hailey, and my grandma is teaching me how to sew with a sewing machine.

MRS. LACEY: Very good. I am very glad to meet all of you.

JOEL: (*raising his hand again, then speaking without being called on*) Mrs. Lacey, Mrs. Lacey......

MRS. LACEY: No Joel. No questions right now. I want to talk about something else right now.

JOEL: (*pointing to Hailey*) ...but how come she didn't say that her wheelchair made her special?

MRS. LACEY: Maybe that's because Hailey doesn't think that her wheelchair is what makes her special.

JOEL: (*not really understanding, he scratches his head*) Oh, OK.

MRS. LACEY: We need to talk about some very important things today. First of all, listening to some of you this morning I have heard some words that are not very nice and maybe even hurtful. We won't be using those words from now on. (*looking directly at the girls in the classroom.*) You know what I'm talking about.

(*Shelly, Robin, and Melissa slap their hands over their mouths.*)

MRS. LACEY: Next on our list is to learn a very important word. (*Mrs. Lacey turns and faces the blackboard. She picks up a piece of chalk and writes in big, block letters, Disability.*) Can anyone tell me what this word is? Anyone, besides Hailey. I know she knows what it is and what it means.

(*Several children try to say the word softly. Some shrug their shoulders, some shake their heads, and others turn and stare at Hailey.*)

MRS. LACEY: (*pointing to each syllable*) Dis-a-bil-i-ty ... Disability. Does anyone know what this word means?

ALL OF THE CHILDRN: No. Nope.

(At the same time Hailey bobs her head up and down.)

HAILEY: Yeah. I know.

JOEL: (*waving his hand in the air*) But Mrs. Lacey, what does that have to do with the new girl, I mean Hailey. What's the matter with her?

MRS. LACEY: (*taking a deep breath*) Well, Joel, as you can all see, Hailey uses a wheelchair. She uses the wheelchair because she has a disability. Her disability is that she can't walk by herself. But Hailey isn't all that different from you and me. You see (*pointing down at her own feet*), I have always had very big feet, and I sometimes trip over them myself. That is my disability. We all have some type of disability. It is just that some of them we can see and some of them we can't see.

(Mrs. Lacey stops, looks around the classroom. The children look confused. She thinks for a moment and then begins again.)

Mrs. Lacey: OK, we all know that Robin wears glasses, right?

ALL OF THE CHILDRN: Yeah. Right.

MRS. LACEY: Well, that is her disability. And we have all seen that Blake wears a hearing aid. Blake's disability is that he doesn't hear as well as the rest of us and his hearing aid helps him hear better.

JOEL: Oh, yeah, huh, I forgot about that.

MRS. LACEY: That's right, Joel. Once you get to know someone, you forget that they have a disability or that they need help in some way. And remember how Shelly always complains that she that she is too short to reach the shelf with the crayons? That is her disability.

(Several of the children shake their heads up and down in agreement.)

SIMON: We help her get stuff down from the tall shelves all the time. It makes her mad that she can't reach things. We don't mind helping her though.

(Mrs. Lacey pauses, looks around the room at the faces of the children as they look at each other with a glimpse of understanding.)

RITA: (*raising her hand*) Mrs. Lacey.

MRS. LACEY: Yes, Rita.

RITA: You mean that a disability is something that doesn't work exactly right?

ROBIN: Or the way it is suppose to, like your feet. You trip 'cause your feet don't work the way they are suppose too because they are too big. I get it now.

MRS. LACEY: *(very excited)* Yes, that is very good Robin and Rita. You see, Anyone can have a disability, but it doesn't really make them any different than you and me. There are all kinds of disabilities. Some you can see and some you can't see.

RITA: That's 'cause nobody's perfect, huh? I know 'cause I have a brother, Simon.

(Simon makes a face at Rita.)

MRS. LACEY: That's right. No one is perfect, Rita.

HAILEY: (shaking her head up and down) And blue is definitely not the perfect color for hair.

(Joel makes a face at Hailey and then laughs at himself, playing with his hair. The rest of the children laugh and agree. The bell rings for recess.)

MRS. LACEY: *(clapping her hands together)* That bell means that it's time for recess.

(Hailey backs away from her deskThe girls look at each other communicating silently.)

MELISSA: Do we have to go outside? We kinda would like to stay in and talk to Hailey and stuff.

MRS. LACEY: *(pleased)* That sounds like a wonderful idea. You go right ahead and get to know each other if you like.

(All of the children stay in the classroom instead of going outside. Hailey moves back from her desk to an open space in the room. The children gather around Hailey. They can't get close enough to her. Some push a little, but they settle down. They start to shoot questions at Hailey faster than she can answer them)

JOEL: How fast can you drive that thing?

RITA: *(pulling at her hair)* I have a disability. Look, my hair is way too curly. It Never works right. I wish it were straight.

SIMON: *(holding up his cast in the back of the group)* Look, I have a real disability. Not made up like Rita. *(pushing to the front)* Hey, I have freckles, too. Is that a disability?

HAILEY: (*beginning to feel like part of the group*)I don't think freckles are a disability. They don't dooooo anything. But curly hair might be.

(Blake and another boy walk around to the back of the wheelchair.)

BLAKE: Hey, check this out! It has two batteries. I bet it's got tons of power. And it can carry a backpack back here, too.

JOEL: *(moving directly in front of Hailey)* Hi, Hailey. I'm Joel. Can I drive your chair?

(Hailey pretends to ignore Joel. All the girls laugh and push Joel out of the way.)

ROBIN: Where did you get that sweater? It's really cool.

HAILEY: At Mervyn's. It was on sale.

SHELLY: Hey, where do you live anyway? *(pointing to several of the girls)* Can We come over after school?

HAILEY: On Locust Ave. But I have to clean my room first. Since we just moved here, my room is kinda messy, and my mom won't let me have company if my room is messy.

RITA: Yeah, mine, too. I wonder how come moms are like that?

(The bell rings for the end of recess. The children start back to their desks. Blake catches up with Joel.)

BLAKE: I wonder what tomorrow's word is going to be?

JOEL: Yeah, this one was way too easy.

(The boys give each other a high five.)

FADE TO BLACK.

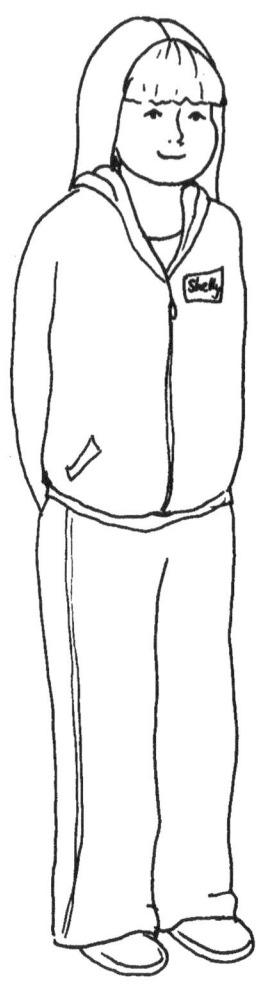

Were You Born In That Chair?

Jennifer Kuhns